PROFESSIONAL EXCELLENCE FOR SECRETARIES

Carolyn Barnes, M.A.
Marilyn Manning, Ph.D.

CRISP PUBLICATIONS, INC.
Los Altos, California

PROFESSIONAL EXCELLENCE FOR SECRETARIES

Carolyn Barnes, M.A.

Marilyn Manning, Ph.D.

CREDITS
Editor: **Michael G. Crisp**
Designer: **Carol Harris**
Typesetting: **Interface Studio**
Cover Design: **Carol Harris**
Artwork: **Ralph Mapson**

Copyright © 1988 by Crisp Publications, Inc.
Printed in the United States of America

Crisp books are distributed in Canada by Reid Publishing, Ltd., P.O. Box 7267, Oakville, Ontario, Canada L6J 6L6.

In Australia by Career Builders, P.O. Box 1051 Springwood, Brisbane, Queensland, Australia 4127.

And in New Zealand by Career Builders, P.O. Box 571, Manurewa, New Zealand.

Library of Congress Catalog Card Number 87-73561
Barnes, Carolyn and Manning, Marilyn
Professional Excellence for Secretaries
ISBN 0-931961-52-1

TO THE READER

Whether your job title reads "Secretary," "Area Associate," "Administrative Assistant," "Executive Assistant," or any number of other descriptions, you are a key member of your organization. In fact, you *are* your organization to many people. For example, when you are on the telephone or responding to a letter you speak for your organization. The age-old saying is true: an office would quickly fall apart without your many skills!

It would be impossible to provide complete guidelines for all the varied secretarial duties in this brief book. Therefore, throughout, we will refer you to other self-study books in the Fifty-Minute Series which cover specific topics in more depth.

This self-study book will help *you* become a *better* secretary. When you make use of its principles and techniques, you will manage your job with less frustration...enjoy your job more and enhance your professional value.

Each section of this book leads you toward better understanding of yourself and your organization and will help you progress toward the goal of professional excellence. The sections are:

Section I —   Understanding the Difference between a Job and a Profession

Section II —   Self Assessment: Your Professional Image

Section III —   Your Role As Office Manager

Section IV —   Your Attitude: The Key to Success with People

Section V —   The Finishing Touch: Becoming a Professional

Section VI —   Your Personal Action Plan

Do you want to avoid last-minute assignments that make you feel frantic? Understand what your manager *really* means when he or she says three different things have top priority? Take your pencil and begin now...You have the control to make each day a step towards professional growth!

Carolyn Barnes
Marilyn Manning

Carolyn Barnes
Marilyn Manning

ABOUT THIS BOOK

PROFESSIONAL EXCELLENCE FOR SECRETARIES is unlike most books. It stands out from other self-help books in an important way. It's not a book to read—it's a book to *use*. The unique "self-paced" format of this book and its worksheets encourage the reader to get involved and try some new ideas immediately.

The objective of this book is to help secretaries assess their present expertise and rise quickly to a new level of personal and professional excellence.

PROFESSIONAL EXCELLENCE FOR SECRETARIES (and the other self-improvement titles listed in the back of this book) can be used effectively in a number of ways. Here are some possibilities:

—**Individual study.** Because the book is self-instructional, all that is needed is a quiet place, some time and a pencil. Completing the activities and exercises will provide valuable feedback, as well as practical ideas for job enhancement.

—**Workshops and Placement Seminars.** This book is ideal for use during, or as pre-assigned reading prior to a workshop or seminar. With the basics in hand, the quality of participation will improve. More time can be spent practicing concept extensions and applications during the program.

—**Informal Study Groups.** Thanks to the format, brevity and low cost, this book is ideal for "brown-bag" or other informal group sessions.

There are other possibilities that depend on the objectives, program or ideas of the user. One thing for sure, even after it has been read, this book will serve as excellent reference material which can be easily reviewed. Good luck!

For more information regarding programs offered by Growth Seminars, Inc., contact Marilyn Manning at 945 Mountain View Ave., Mountain View, California (415) 965-3663.

CONTENTS

SECTION I

DOING A PROFESSIONAL JOB

The difference between a clerk and a world-class secretary (or associate, or administrative assistant, or executive secretary) is a combination of personal confidence, polished skills, and a global, rather than task-oriented approach to each day's possibilities.

As you work toward professional excellence, it is often helpful to model your behavior after someone you respect.

You will discover that highly successful employees have much in common. More than anything else, they share

—a thorough knowledge of their organization:
    its goals, products, service
    its employees, clients (customers), executives
    its history
    its future possibilities

—plus, an ability to perform each task so that the organization
    as a whole is best served (this is called *global orientation*).

Secretaries who concentrate on single tasks and never see ''the bigger picture'' are clerk-level workers. Some examples of task-oriented and global-oriented behaviors are presented on the facing page.

IT'S YOUR CHOICE!

PROFESSIONAL BEHAVIORS	TASK-ORIENTED BEHAVIORS

Is sensitive to the "rhythm" of the boss' day and groups questions at convenient times.

Interrupts boss whenever help is needed with individual tasks.

Updates and monitors files, reflecting current needs of office personnel.

Keeps files the way they've always been, because it is easier.

Notices changed addresses and phone numbers on incoming mail. Makes appropriate changes immediately.

Changes nothing unless instructed by a manager.

Notices when many correspondents ask similar questions and drafts a model response letter to become more efficient.

Answers each letter or request individually, without noting patterns or trends.

Recognizes phone calls from unhappy customers as an opportunity to suggest improvements in company policies.

Dreads phone calls from unhappy customers because of not knowing what to say.

When another department requests assistance, helps (or finds help) as soon as possible.

Delays other department's requests "so they learn to do their own work."

When working on a project, is happy to insert last-minute changes, even if it means considerable additional work.

Once a project has begun, refuses to alter its format or schedule.

Add your own:

_____

_____

_____

Working with other secretaries, you have had the opportunity to observe contributions they have made, ways they have significantly helped their organization. List two which you recall:

1. _____

2. _____

YOUR ATTITUDE AND YOUR JOB

> The "magic key" that opens your mind
> and heart to better job performance—and a
> better life—is YOUR ATTITUDE!

A positive attitude helps you:

—Consider your job as part of the larger pattern of your entire organization.

—Visualize your potential when dealing with other employees, customers, and clients.

—Understand how your attitude affects other people's attitudes and performances.

Your skill in dealing with others is your most important asset! This book will show you how to approach every specific task or duty with a positive attitude that will make you a professional.

WHO IS A PROFESSIONAL?

"Professional" refers to an attitude, not necessarily a job description. The *professional* worker:

—takes the job seriously, seeing it as important in his or her career plan.

—cares enough to analyze how the job could be performed better even if it means making changes.

—understands how the job relates to the organization as a whole.

—feels confident about sharing ideas, goals, enthusiasm with other people.

YOUR PROFESSIONAL ATTITUDE ENHANCES ALL YOUR OTHER SKILLS AND ENABLES YOU TO USE THEM MORE EFFECTIVELY.

YOUR ATTITUDE TOWARD BEING A SECRETARY

To measure your attitude, please complete this exercise. Read the statement and circle athe number where you feel you belong. If you circle a 5, you are saying your attitude could not be better in this area; if you circle a 1, you are saying being a professional secretary may not be for you.

	Agree				Disagree
I seek responsibility.	5	4	3	2	1
Becoming a respected secretary is important to me.	5	4	3	2	1
I enjoy helping others do a good job.	5	4	3	2	1
I want to know more about human behavior.	5	4	3	2	1
I want to advance in my career.	5	4	3	2	1
I am anxious to learn and master secretarial skills.	5	4	3	2	1
I like leadership situations.	5	4	3	2	1
Working with a problem employee would be an interesting challenge.	5	4	3	2	1
I intend to devote time to learn motivational skills	5	4	3	2	1
I'm excited about the opportunity to become a professional secretary.	5	4	3	2	1

TOTAL

If you scored above 40, you have an excellent attitude toward becoming a professional secretary. If you rated yourself between 25 and 40, it would appear you have a few reservations. A rating under 25 indicates you should rethink pursuing a career as a secretary.

This scale was adapted from THE FIFTY-MINUTE SUPERVISOR by Elwood N. Chapman. For order information see the back of this book.

WHAT IS AN OFFICE, ANYWAY?

There are offices everywhere in the world, from Australia to Zambia. And in every office, someone will be:

—Typing and filing

—Keeping office records and reports

—Screening telephone calls

—(Probably!) Using a copy machine

—Organizing a filing system.

WHY?

An office is *not* an end in itself. It is a "service" department which is supposed to make the work of others more effective. Here are examples of work which offices support:

—product development and production

—wholesale and retail sales

—teaching and academic administration

—health care delivery

—legal services

—government programs (local, state, national)

—arts and entertainment

—

— (Add your own examples)

—

AN OFFICE EXISTS TO SERVE ITS WORKERS,
CUSTOMERS, AND CLIENTS

BUT

THE NEEDS OF WORKERS, CUSTOMERS, AND CLIENTS
ARE ALWAYS CHANGING!

USE A GLOBAL ORIENTATION TO ANALYZE YOUR OFFICE

1. The work which my office supports is _____

2. Our customers or clients are _____

3. Our main competitors are _____

   _____

4. As an office we are doing better (___) or worse (___) than last year

   because _____

   and _____

5. Ways in which our business or organization has changed in the past several months:

   _____

   _____

   _____

6. Changes in our basic business which have caused changes in our office procedures:

   _____

   _____

   _____

7. Ways I feel our office needs to change to *better* support our customers or clients:

   _____

   _____

   _____

> BEING SUCCESSFUL MEANS SEEING YOURSELF AS VITAL TO YOUR ORGANIZATION'S PROGRESS.
> YOU CAN BE THE FIRST TO NOTICE POSSIBILITIES FOR CHANGE AND IMPROVEMENT!

TRANSLATING IDEAS INTO ACTION

Here are some tips that should help you feel comfortable about moving toward a more professional approach to your work.

People often claim they don't like "being in a rut," but then fight actual changes in their work methods. It is only natural to fear unknown consequences when you change your behavior. If this book gives you twenty ideas for managing your job differently, *only you* will know them. And you can decide, step by step, when and how you will put them into action.

Some people believe "changing their image" means not being true to who they really are. Professional growth comes when new ideas lead to new ways of seeing. If you look around your office and notice that people who are not dressed professionally (i.e. wearing jeans) are not taken seriously, it makes sense to be aware of your appearance.

The "us" v.s. "them" mentality among administrative staff is very strong in some offices (particularly large offices). The support staff often will feel loyalty to each other, rather than to the organization as a whole. This attitude stops professional growth, yet can seem comfortable and safe on a day-by-day basis.

MAKING CHANGES SMOOTHLY

1. Change one thing at a time—slow and easy does it.

2. Define your goal in simple, active, positive words.

3. Write your change goal and post it where you see it daily.

4. If your change affects other people, tell them what you plan to do and why. Discuss your goal. If they have other ideas, listen. The discussion itself may lead to a better working relationship.

5. A great deal of practice may be needed before a new behavior becomes natural. Remember, you don't have to be perfect every time!

DEMONSTRATE YOUR PROGRESS

For each statement below, put a check under TRUE or FALSE when you think you know the answer.

TRUE   FALSE

_____ _____   1.   A professional secretary thinks globally and sees his/her office as part of the organization as a whole.

_____ _____   2.   Thinking globally means looking for new ways to serve customers or clients more efficiently.

_____ _____   3.   A secretary who is task-oriented concentrates only on the job at hand, and is annoyed at interruptions.

_____ _____   4.   The professional knows the history of his/her organization and the possibilities for its future.

_____ _____   5.   An office should have set rules and procedures that do not change.

_____ _____   6.   A positive attitude doesn't really matter on the job.

_____ _____   7.   Upgrading one's clothing and grooming is a way of showing off.

_____ _____   8.   An employee who suggests changes should be viewed with suspicion by fellow employees.

IF YOU UNDERSTAND THE PURPOSE AND GOALS OF YOUR ORGANIZATION, YOU CAN LOOK FOR WAYS TO MAKE YOUR OFFICE MORE EFFICIENT AND SUPPORTIVE...AND MAKE YOURSELF AN INVALUABLE ASSET.

ANSWERS: 1-4 are true; 5-8, false.

SECTION II

SELF-ASSESSMENT

YOUR PROFESSIONAL IMAGE: WHAT IS IT TODAY?

"I am a very important part of my manager's administrative team who can be relied on in any emergency." (A secretary quoted in *Working Woman* magazine)

"My secretary is a sales representative, customer-service expert, quality-control inspector, data-processing coordinator, and too many additional things to list here." (A company vice-president quoted in the same article)

How do you see yourself in your job?

Do other people see you the same way?

Flexibility is a key quality in order to meet your manager's and organization's ever-changing needs. Each day pressures and adjustments will require your ability to re-prioritize in order to complete the most important tasks. In time, within the framework of your particular job, you will develop your own areas of expertise. Chances are, you will find your job responsibilities growing at the same rate as your personal confidence level. A professional secretary is a key player on the office team. Often it is he or she who really "makes things happen."

The following profiles (all true stories!) show secretaries in action. Which is most like you? Are you harvesting the highest personal growth potential from your job?

PROFILE I

WILLIAM

William's office skills are adequate, although his writing and spelling ability is poor. He hangs a comic "calendar" over his desk. It shows crazed, depressed, or sleeping figures in the boxes for Monday through Thursday, and laughing, happy figures on Friday, Saturday, and Sunday. On his computer, he places a little statue holding a flag that says, "Think Friday." He's often fifteen or twenty minutes late in the morning. When he arrives, his hair is wet from the shower, and he is munching a donut he bought on the way to work. When given added responsibilities, he doesn't finish on time or do a complete job, unless reminded and prodded by the manager. He has never suggested additional duties for himself. He tells his friends he would like a more interesting job and better pay.

What advice would you give to William? _____

_____

_____

_____

_____

_____

_____

_____

_____

_____

PROFILE II

> **MARILYN**
>
> Marilyn did not work outside of her home for twelve years while her children were young. Once she decided to return to the workplace she attended the local community college to update her office skills. Once she felt confident with her basic skills she began interviewing for a job and was soon hired by a local realty firm. She wants to eventually study for a real estate license and has already begun to take courses.

How could Marilyn manage her job to achieve her personal goals?

_____

_____

_____

Would these changes improve or detract from her professional image as the company secretary?

_____

_____

_____

_____

_____

_____

_____

_____

PROFILE III

HEATHER

Heather decided to accept a job in a bank because she always enjoyed working with figures and was intrigued with investments. She started as a temporary secretary at the headquarters of an international bank and became a permanent employee after six months. In the past eight years, she has worked in virtually every department of the bank. She is currently the assistant to the president, supervising an elegant two-floor suite that was filmed in a James Bond movie. She composes and types most of the president's letters and memos. She has developed a sizable investment portfolio, based on opportunities discovered through her research for bank reports.

Was Heather just lucky? Can you guess at some of the traits which enabled her to rise to her current position in the organization?

_____

_____

_____

_____

_____

_____

_____

_____

_____

WHERE ARE *YOU* NOW?

WILLIAM, MARILYN, AND HEATHER ALL STARTED WITH THE SAME
GENERAL JOB DESCRIPTION—BUT EACH PERSON CHOSE INDIVIDUAL
GOALS and
ATTITUDES.

How can you manage *your* job to best meet *your personal goals?*

First you have to assess what they are! Below are some questions to get you
started. Remember: be honest with yourself. No one else will be affected by your
answers but YOU!

1. Do you have a clear picture of where you are going with your
    professional life during the next five years?   ( ) yes   ( ) no

2. Do others (i.e. your supervisor/subordinates) know about your plans?
    ( ) yes   ( ) no

3. Have you set specific targets for your personal life for the next five
    years?   ( ) yes   ( ) no

4. Do those you count on for support (family, close friends, etc.) know
    about these targets?   ( ) yes   ( ) no

5. Are you totally satisfied with the progress you are making in your
    professional life?   ( ) yes   ( ) no

6. Are you satisfied with your life progress?
    ( ) yes   ( ) no

7. Do you have a written method to track your professional and personal
    progress?   ( ) yes   ( ) no

8. Are your underlying values clear and sharp in your mind?
    ( ) yes   ( ) no

9. Have you written them down?   ( ) yes   ( ) no

Because an administrative position is usually flexible, within certain limitations,
you have the power to make your job work FOR YOU. You can test and challenge
yourself, and grow professionally and personally.

This self-test was adapted from SUCCESSFUL SELF-MANAGEMENT: A Psychologically Sound
Approach to Personal Effectiveness, by Paul R. Timm, Ph.D. For order information, see the back of
the book.

Professional Excellence for Secretaries

WHAT CAN *SUCCESS* AS A PROFESSIONAL SECRETARY DO FOR YOU?

Many good things can happen once you become a top-flight secretary. Ten statements are listed below. Three are false. Place a check in the square opposite these false statements and match your answers with those of the authors at the bottom of the page.

With greater professionalism I will:

☐   1. Increase my earnings potential.

☐   2. Have opportunities to learn more.

☐   3. Develop an ulcer.

☐   4. Position myself for promotions.

☐   5. Have less freedom.

☐   6. Increase my self-confidence.

☐   7. Try out my leadership wings.

☐   8. Have fewer friends.

☐   9. Learn and develop human relations skills.

☐ 10. Have better feelings of self worth.

You will find the answers to this exercise at the bottom of the page.

False Statements

3. There is no evidence that top-flight secretaries have more ulcers than other employees.

5. The professional secretary generally has *more* freedom, because she is trusted with far more authority by her boss.

8. Professional secretaries develop new friends and keep the old ones.

Adapted from THE FIFTY-MINUTE SUPERVISOR: A Guide for the Newly Promoted, by Elwood N. Chapman. For order information, see the back of this book.

SECTION III

YOUR ROLE AS OFFICE MANAGER

Whether your "office" consists of just you and your boss, or of a large number of other people, your office managing skills will set the climate for everyone. You can help others achieve better performance.

You are especially valuable to your organization because you juggle many tasks at once. Computers and office technology will never make your job obsolete. In fact, the United States Bureau of Labor Statistics projects a 13.1 *increase* in secretarial jobs between 1986 and 2000. (In contrast, the Bureau projects a 13.9 percent decrease in the number of typists and word processors and a 28.2 percent decrease in the number of stenographers.) Single task occupations *can* be phased out, but the diverse role of secretary/administrative assistant remains vital.

Your administrative role requires you to establish priorities, coordinate projects, and organize resources. As "office manager", your professional attitude and behavior greatly influences each day's accomplishments.

GETTING ORGANIZED

The first step toward control of your managerial duties is to list all of your office tasks and then rate them. Use the chart on the next page to determine your priorities.

RATING TASKS AND SETTING PRIORITIES

IDENTIFY TASKS AND ACTIVITIES: List your tasks and activities at work. If you have difficulty remembering them, just close your eyes and see yourself in your work space, doing your job. Notice the various tasks and activities. Do you answer the phone? Complete forms? Answer letters? List them below.

RATE IMPACT: Using a scale from 1 to 10, with 1 being ''no impact'' and 10 being ''great impact,'' rate the impact that each activity has upon performance of your job.

ASSIGN PRIORITIES: Use the impact ratings to assign priorities to each task or activity. Assign as ''A'' priority for tasks with ratings over 7; ''B'' priority for ratings from 4 to 6; and ''C'' priority for ratings below 3.

SCHEDULE: Use your priority rating system to schedule your day. Start with ''A'' tasks and activities. Try scheduling them directly on your calendar. Leave ''C'' priorities until last and, whenever possible, delegate them. What would happen if you didn't do the ''C'' activity at all? DISCUSS YOUR OPINIONS WITH YOUR SUPERVISOR AND ASK FOR IDEAS ABOUT THE BEST USE OF YOUR TIME.

Task/Activity	Impact	Priority
(Example) Keeping correspondence filed in chronological order.	A	7

MAKE AN APPOINTMENT TODAY TO DISCUSS YOUR IDEAS WITH YOUR MANAGER!

(Rating sheet adapted from PREVENTING JOB BURNOUT by Beverly A. Potter, Ph.D. For order information, see the back of the book.)

EVERY DAY YOU ARE A
TIME MANAGER

Successful secretaries are expert time managers. To reach your goals, you must prioritize responsibilities, finish tasks completely, create schedules—and stick to them.

SECRETS OF TIME MANAGEMENT

—Do top priority tasks first.

—Divide big jobs into manageable steps (a special calendar for a big project may be helpful).

—Use a timetable, and be sure to use workable units.

—Do one thing at a time.

—Finish tasks completely (or use very good notes to yourself so that you don't waste time when you return).

—Do it *now*!

MARK POSTPONES THE PROMOTION REPORT

Mark, as assistant to the vice-president in charge of marketing, was asked to prepare a report summarizing the results of the last three years from a promotion letter sent each spring and recommending changes to this year's letter. Mark has the necessary research materials filed in the office, but somehow has not found the right moment to start the report. Now there are only three weeks before the promotion letter should be sent out. What should Mark do?

_____

_____

_____

_____

_____

GROUPING SIMILAR ACTIVITIES AND PLANNING FOR FUTURE NEEDS

When you consider your daily schedule, you may find that it reflects your past experience at another job, or perhaps developed by chance, as you learned your present job. One exercise that will help you re-evaluate your schedule is to imagine explaining your routine to an inexperienced visitor. Does it make sense? Have you ever really considered *why* you do certain things at certain times of the day? Following are some ideas which may make you more efficient.

GROUP TASKS FOR GREATER EFFICIENCY:

1. Make out-going telephone calls in groups. Time them when most people can be reached. Use notes to guide each conversation and make notes about responses and/or any follow-up action that is required.

2. Sort and prioritize the mail into specific groups (i.e. immediate action by boss, "I can handle," information, junk, etc.).

3. Draft replies to incoming letters immediately after opening and sorting the mail.

4. Transcribe letters during a specific morning or afternoon hour.

5. Stock supplies once a week, rather than running to the supply closet or requisitioning items every day.

6. If you have assistants, give them all their work and instructions at one time, rather than for each separate job. Set a regular time for them to bring completed work to you.

7. Prepare the outgoing mail throughout the day rather than leaving it all until the last minute and perhaps missing the last pickup.

8. Make a checklist and organize every step of a major mailing at one time, so that all necessary letterheads, forms, envelopes, enclosures, etc., can be ordered simultaneously.

9. At the end of each day, take a few minutes to organize a "To-Do" list for the following day, with subjects such as: Mail, Reports, Telephone Calls, Appointments, Internal Follow-ups. If you wait until tomorrow to make your list, it will take longer and you will run the risk of forgetting something important.

YOUR IDEAS FOR A DIFFERENT WORK SCHEDULE

1. Tasks which should be done in the first hour:

    _____

    _____

    _____

    _____

2. Tasks for the half-hour before lunch:

    _____

    _____

    _____

    _____

3. Tasks for immediately after lunch:

    _____

    _____

    _____

    _____

4. End-of-the-day tasks:

    _____

    _____

    _____

    _____

LONG-RANGE OFFICE PLANNING

Professional secretaries adopt the same office planning viewpoint as managers. Office activities are anticipated, planned, and coordinated on a long-range basis. The overall pattern of your job should be structured according to your manager's long-term goals.

You and your manager must work together on this. Only by becoming active partners and communicating objectives and needs will you be in a position to turn goals into realities.

SET THE SCENE FOR LONG-RANGE PLANNING

1. First make a list of reports or projects that occur annually, semi-annually, quarterly, monthly, and weekly. Place this information on a calendar or time line chart.

2. Next, indicate time periods on the chart which are normally hectic.

3. Note any scheduled trips, vacation periods, holidays, etc.

4. Fill in regular meetings and appointments which can be predicted.

5. Once you have completed the above, you should have a ''year at a glance'' planning document to review with your manager. A meeting (or series of meetings) between the two of you can assign priorities, establish schedules and deadlines, etc.

6. Monthly and weekly planning (using the above steps) will provide a realistic look at major activities and prevent or minimize the last-minute ''frantics.''

LONG RANGE
PLANNING (Continued)

WHAT ARE THE BEST TIMES FOR YOU AND THE BOSS TO PLAN OR
REVIEW LONG-RANGE GOALS? HAVE YOU SCHEDULED A MEETING TO
DISCUSS THEM?

_____

_____

_____

LIST ALL MAJOR LONG-RANGE GOALS THE OFFICE NEEDS TO CONSIDER
AND ACCOMPLISH:

_____

_____

_____

_____

_____

WHAT STEPS MUST YOU TAKE TO TRANSFORM THREE OF THE MAJOR
LONG-RANGE GOALS INTO REALITY?

_____

_____

_____

_____

_____

MYTHS AND MISCONCEPTIONS ABOUT TIME

(Or, why you need to be organized NOW!)

1. The pressure will end someday.

2. Coming in early, working late or working on weekends will end job pressure.

3. People will someday stop asking for things at the last minute.

4. There will be predictable blocks of uninterrupted time each day.

CAN YOU ADD OTHERS THAT YOU ONCE BELIEVED OR EVEN COUNTED ON?

_____

_____

_____

_____

_____

5 STEPS TO IMPROVE YOUR DECISION MAKING

PROFESSIONAL SECRETARIES ARE NOT AFRAID TO MAKE DECISIONS. The types of decisions you make as a secretary are different from those made by a manager or a company president, but the process is identical. Good decisions are based on more than luck. If a person understands the process, quality decisions can be made. *If you are decisive, you are much more valuable to your organization.*

FOLLOWING ARE FIVE STEPS TO BETTER DECISION MAKING. With each step, an example is included for illustration:

1. **GATHER INFORMATION.** Be well-informed. Learn the facts. Talk to other people. *(Example: Jennie needed to decide which of two software programs would handle the travel records for nine company sales reps. She asked other departments for their recommendations. She visited retail software stores and talked to their salespeople. She read reviews of each program and kept notes of her findings.)*

2. **EVALUATE THE INFORMATION.** Which facts are relevant to the situation? What are this organization's values? *(For instance, is saving money on equipment more important than getting the latest refinements? How many people will use this particular program and how skilled are they?)*

3. **RECOGNIZE THE CONSEQUENCES OF EACH ALTERNATIVE.** *(Example: If Jennie bought one program, it would not run it on all the computers in her office. If she bought the other program, it could not accommodate all of the categories she needed to record. Neither program fulfilled all of her office needs.)*

4. **MAKE A DECISION AND INFORM OTHERS OF IT.** Even when a decision is difficult you should inform those directly involved about the decision you plan to make, summarizing the pros and cons. *(Example: Jennie elected to select the program that could accommodate all of the needed travel categories.)*

5. **TAKE ACTION ON YOUR DECISION.** (The actual decision occurs when you act upon it.) *Example: Jennie's purchase of one computer program illustrates taking action on the decision.*

RATE YOUR DECISION-MAKING

DESCRIBE A DECISION YOU MADE RECENTLY:

_____

_____

DID YOU GATHER INFORMATION? _____

DID YOU EVALUATE THE INFORMATION? _____

WHAT ALTERNATIVES DID YOU CONSIDER?

_____

_____

HOW DID YOU RECOGNIZE THE CONSEQUENCES OF EACH
ALTERNATIVE? (Explain) _____

_____

DID YOU INFORM OTHERS OF YOUR DECISION? _____

_____

_____

ARE YOU HAPPY WITH YOUR DECISION? _____

WHAT (IF ANYTHING) DO YOU PLAN TO DO DIFFERENTLY WITH YOUR
NEXT DECISION? _____

_____

DO YOU FEEL YOU ARE MAKING MORE IMPORTANT DECISIONS NOW
THAN YOU WERE LAST YEAR?

(YES) _____(NO) _____WHY? _____

_____

THE MORE DECISIONS YOU MAKE, THE GREATER YOUR SKILL AND
SELF CONFIDENCE. WELCOME THE CHANCE TO MAKE DECISIONS!

DECISION MAKING CHECKLIST

Use the format shown below to help you make your next decision.

DECISION TO BE MADE

_____

1. I will GATHER INFORMATION from _____
   _____ (people); and _____
   _____ (other sources).

2. I will EVALUATE THE INFORMATION by _____
   _____
   _____ (checking its relevancy, my values,
   considering timing needs).

3. THE CONSEQUENCES OF EACH OF MY ALTERNATIVES ARE:
   ALTERNATIVE 1 _____
   ALTERNATIVE 2 _____
   ALTERNATIVE 3 _____

4. I will communicate my decision to: _____
   _____
   _____

5. My decision is: _____
   _____
   _____

WHEN YOU HAVE DIFFICULTY MAKING A DECISION AT THE OFFICE
OR IN YOUR PERSONAL LIFE, REFER TO THIS PAGE AND FOLLOW
THESE STEPS. *REMEMBER: EVERY DECISION YOU MAKE DOESN'T
HAVE TO BE PERFECT!*

THE PROBLEM OF WORK OVERLOAD

Do you often feel overloaded with work? If so, a major reason may be your boss does not understand how long certain tasks take, or may be unaware of other duties which must be performed at the same time.

Communication and *Attitude* are the keys here. When you view work overload as a challenge, rather than a problem, solutions will come more easily. If you do not communicate (and document) the problem, however, your overload will become the rule and not the exception. Make sure you discuss overload problems with your boss after you have done the following:

1. Keep a written record of work requests, deadlines, time approximations vs time actually spent. (Perhaps in a special notebook.)

2. If your supervisor interrupts you with several new work requests, take out your notebook, and ask which project can be delayed.

3. Stay aware of (and suggest) other help that might be available (from someone else in the office, an outside service, etc.).

4. Or, recommend that you start work on the latest request, and let someone else do an earlier job.

5. Do not hesitate to ask questions about juggling deadlines, or work priorities. IT IS BETTER TO BE A QUESTION ASKER THAN A MISTAKE MAKER.

6. If you find yourself getting frustrated and angry about work overload, it is easy to look like a complainer. BE POSITIVE AND ORGANIZED! Keep your work assignment notebook up-to-date and communicate any problems as they occur.

CASE STUDY

CASE STUDY

LINDA LEARNS THE ROPES (WITH YOUR HELP)

Linda's manager, a TV producer, receives a steady stream of telephone calls daily. This person also requires extensive help with correspondence. The producer asks Linda to coordinate an upcoming meeting of other network producers, requiring much telephone work, the drafting of a preliminary agenda, the reproduction of various fact sheets, as well as taking notes at the meeting itself. This is a new job for Linda, and she doesn't know where to begin. What should she say to the producer and how should she plan her workload?

UPDATING YOUR OFFICE SKILLS

When you view yourself as an office manager rather than a secretary, your fields of professional study can lead in exciting new directions. Your expertise should begin with a basic mastery of office skills, but can go far beyond. Whatever your background, chances are there are new procedures and skills that would help you do a better job. Consider the following areas when you explore office or college course descriptions:

> —Office Administration
> —Office Technology and Applications Software
> —Business Economics
> —Financial Analysis and Management
> —Marketing
> —Management
> —Accounting
> —Business Law
> —Communications (Speaking, Writing)

Many companies have programs that pay tuition costs for employees who take night or weekend courses and workshops. Large organizations also often have in-house training programs offered on a regular basis.

Do you know what educational opportunities are offered by your employer? Are you aware of classes which would help you professionally that are available at your local schools and colleges?

BE A DECISION MAKER AND PROBLEM SOLVER.
LOOK FOR CLASSES TO ENHANCE YOUR SKILLS!

(Don't forget to give yourself credit for reading this book!)

PROFESSIONAL ORGANIZATIONS FOR SECRETARIES

Secretaries are sometimes unaware of the professional organizations which exist to promote better recognition on the job and to certify their skills. Professional Secretaries International represents more than 40,000 secretaries and offers a Certified Professional Secretary (CPS) credential that certifies a minimum level of skills.

To qualify, candidates must take a two-day exam that tests knowledge of economics and management, accounting, business law, behavioral sciences, office technology and administration and communication. The complete six-part test costs about $100 for PSI members and $125 for non-members. PSI has made five-year re-certification mandatory for new recipients. For more information, write Professional Secretaries International, 301 East Armour Blvd., Kansas City, MO, 64111-1299.

Other professional organizations which promote professional excellence:

American Business Women's Association
9100 Ward Parkway
P.O. Box 8728
Kansas City, MO 64114
Teaches leadership skills, encourages continuing education, provides workshops and seminars, awards over $3 million in scholarships annually. 110,000 members.

American Society of Professional and Executive Women
1511 Walnut Street
Philadelphia, PA 19102

Provides library services, recruitment data bank, resume guide, publications, conducts seminars. 12,400 members.

The National Federation of Business and Professional Women's Clubs, Inc.
2012 Massachusetts Ave., N.W.
Washington, D.C. 20036
Provides leadership training, career related seminars. Offers networking opportunities. 141,000 members.

The National Association of Female Executives
1031 Third Avenue
New York, NY 10021
A major association dedicated to professional growth for female employees.

In Australia, contact The Institute of Professional Secretaries
P.O. Box 3167
Syndey, NSW 2001

THE IMPORTANCE OF ACQUIRING HIGH QUALITY COMMUNICATION SKILLS

The next three topics are of special importance because they reflect the times *you are the voice your organization to other people.* When you write letters, speak on the telephone, or make oral presentations you represent your organization. By assessing your present level of confidence in these areas, you can identify where additional study and practice would be helpful.

Good communication skills make every other part of your job easier!

Keep these general principles in mind, whenever you are writing *or* speaking:

1. There is no substitute for knowing the facts about your subject. Learn everything you can about your organization, how it works, who does what job, normal schedules and procedures, general policies, which customers or clients warrant special consideration.

2. Never be afraid to say or write that you do not know something. Do say, however, that you will find out and let the other person know as soon as possible. *Then be sure to follow through on your promise.*

3. Always try to understand the other person's point of view: what is he or she really asking? LISTEN to the other person or read his/her letter carefully, and consider the context form from which it was written.

4. When unpleasant information must be communicated, soften it with something positive.

5. Observe how effective people around you use the telephone. Ask to read samples of their correspondence. What works well for them? How could you adapt their methods to work for you?

   Use your imagination!

TELEPHONE COURTESY

EFFECTIVE PRESENTATION SKILLS

BETTER BUSINESS WRITING

WRITING WITH CONFIDENCE

Many managers and executives understand that the highest paid secretaries and associates are among the world's best ghost writers! The better your communication skills (especially writing), the more time you save your manager...and the more valuable you become. Rate yourself as a writer by answering the following questions:

YES   NO

____ ____ 1. I always keep my audience in mind when I write. (Are they men? women? Do they want to know every fact or just the "bottom line"?)

____ ____ 2. I have no problem with the basics: grammar, spelling, and punctuation. (If your answer is "no", buy a secretarial handbook and dictionary and take a brush-up class.)

____ ____ 3. I know the difference between active and passive construction, and try to use the active wherever possible. (Examples: Passive—The secretary was hired by Mary. Active—Mary hired the secretary.)

____ ____ 4. I choose simple words to communicate clearly.
Complex: Subsequently, we'll require your endorsement.
Simple: Later, we'll need your signature.

____ ____ 5. I make it a point to state clearly the specific purpose of my letters or memos. (Preferably, in simple words in the first paragraph.)

____ ____ 6. I keep a file of sample letters so I can quickly put together an appropriate response to the routine letters we receive.

____ ____ 7. I personalize letters so the recipient will feel recognized.

____ ____ 8. If there is any doubt about how a name is spelled, I double-check it. I understand how important a person's name and/or title is.

____ ____ 9. I know that it is hard to proofread my own work, so I have a "buddy" in the office with whom I exchange important letters, reports, etc.

Every "yes" makes you a better business writer!

Two excellent self-study books on business writing are BETTER BUSINESS WRITING by Susan L. Brock and WRITING FITNESS by Jack Swenson. (Both may be ordered using the form on page 73).

MAKE EVERY LETTER A SALES LETTER

The cost to an organization of an original one-page letter is estimated at more than twenty dollars when all office expenses are considered! It is therefore very important to make sure that your letters are professional in content and appearance and support your organization.

EVERY LETTER THAT LEAVES YOUR OFFICE IS A "SALES LETTER". THIS IS BECAUSE IT REPRESENTS YOUR MANAGER OR YOUR COMPANY. YOU CAN MAKE OR BREAK IMPORTANT FUTURE BUSINESS BY THE WAY YOU HANDLE WRITTEN CORRESPONDENCE.

WHAT MAKES A *BAD* LETTER?

HERE ARE TEN EASY WAYS TO MAKE A LETTER READER *REALLY MAD*:

1. Ramble around the subject so it's difficult to tell what the letter is trying to say.

2. Fail to answer any questions asked in a previous letter.

3. Spell the recipient's name wrong; get the address scrambled; assume an incorrect title or sex, or be too "familiar."

4. Sound demanding, selfish, superior, or talk down to your reader.

5. Use cliché after cliché, with nothing original or personal.

6. Forget to send a reply card or return envelope when you request a quick answer.

7. Don't provide a telephone number when you ask for a return call.

8. Use small-sized or faintly printed type, so your letter is a real strain to read.

9. Have noticable strike-overs or erasures.

10. Refuse to have someone proof-read your letter.

Take your letter-writing *very seriously indeed*. You *are* your organization to your reader.

PROFESSIONAL TELEPHONE TECHNIQUES

Another place (besides letters) where you are the voice of your organization is on the telephone. You represent your manager and your company every time you answer the phone. Take the quiz below to test your skill and confidence:

True or False

_____ 1. It is okay to keep someone waiting on the phone while you attend to another equally important task.

_____ 2. You should actually smile when you answer the telephone.

_____ 3. If nobody is around to answer a ringing phone and it is not your assigned job, the best thing to do is to let it ring.

_____ 4. It is acceptable to not return a call. If the call was important, the calling party will try again.

_____ 5. If a caller is rude, it is your right to be equally snippy.

_____ 6. You should identify yourself by name when answering a business related telephone call.

_____ 7. If business is slow, it is perfectly acceptable to make personal calls to your friends.

_____ 8. It is important to communicate a sincere interest in the caller and the information that is being requested or provided.

_____ 9. The conversation should be ended in an upbeat manner, with a summary of any action to be taken.

_____ 10. When you are upset, it is possible to communicate a negative attitude over the phone without realizing it.

| ANSWERS: | 1)F | 2)T | 3)F | 4)F | 5)F | 6)T | 7)F | 8)T | 9)T | 10)T |

This quiz is adapted from *TELEPHONE COURTESY AND CUSTOMER SERVICE* by Lloyd Finch. For order information, see the back of the book.

EFFECTIVE PRESENTATION SKILLS

As a secretary there will be many opportunities for oral communication. For example, attending a meeting…hosting visiting salespeople…or explaining your secretarial duties to trainees can lead to public speaking in many different settings. Following is a typical example of presenting information to a group of colleagues:

JILL

Jill is invited, along with her manager, to attend a meeting of all department heads in the company. She is not expecting to say anything, only to sit and listen. During her manager's presentation, he is asked a question about the department's plans for the coming year. He turns to Jill and says, ''Jill, you've been working on this project while I've been away. Maybe you could say a few words about how this project got started, where it stands and where it is going.''

If something like this happens to you, don't panic! You know how to organize your thoughts and you know your job. With these two resources you can effectively respond by taking the following steps:

FIRST, THINK!

Use your organizational skills. Any topic can be split into components. Before you speak, break your topic into a pattern such as:

A) past, present and future (or any time-oriented combination),

B) topic 1, 2, and 3 (e.g. production, advertising, and marketing),

C) the pros and cons of an issue (useful in persuasive situations). In Jill's case above, the time-ordered sequence fits right in.

THEN SPEAK:

1. *Give a few introductory remarks.*
    Before you launch into the meat of your topic, give yourself time to get collected. Make some general introductory comments, such as, *''Thanks, boss, I'm pleased to be here today to help provide some information. I didn't plan a formal presentation but would be happy to describe the project we've been working on.''*

EFFECTIVE PRESENTATION SKILLS
(Continued)

2. *Develop a clear preview sentence of your main points.*

   You will want to verbalize to yourself and your audience what your key points are. From the example above Jill could simply state, *"I would like to tell you about how we started this project, where it stands and where we plan to take it."* This is a time ordered sequence.

3. *Deliver the body of the presentation.*

   Talk through each point from your preview sentence. (In Jill's example; past, present and future). Having an organizational pattern established and knowing where you are going will take some of the stress out of the situation.

   If what you are speaking about is controversial, first acknowledge the opposition's case but finish with your viewpoint so you end by summarizing your position.

4. *Review the main points.*

   Reinforce the main ideas you've touched upon by briefly restating them. Something like, *"I've tried in these past few minutes to give you an overview of how this project started, where it is now and where we think it will go."*

5. *Conclude the presentation.*

   Don't leave your presentation high and dry. Conclude it with a strong, positive, statement. Following our example, *"I hope to attend next month's meeting to report a satisfactory conclusion to our project. I would be happy to take any questions at this time."*

Professional Excellence for Secretaries

If you find yourself regularly being called upon to contribute at meetings, you will find many helpful ideas in EFFECTIVE PRESENTATION SKILLS: A Practical Guide for Better Speaking by Steve Mandel. For order information, see the back of the book. (The above impromptu speaking guide was adapted from Mr. Mandel's book.)

PLANNING FOR MEETINGS

Whether your supervisor is hosting a meeting or attending one elsewhere, your assistance will play a significant role in how productive the meeting will be.

WHEN YOU AND YOUR SUPERVISOR ARE PLANNING THE MEETING

1. Set up a checklist of pre-meeting arrangements, such as room reservations, audio-visual rental, food requirements, budget considerations, etc.

2. Send written announcements to all participants (with an enclosed agenda when possible).

3. Enclose RSVP postcards, a phone number or more elaborate reply cards, depending on tradition and how important the meeting will be.

4. Be sure to follow-up with phone calls if people have not replied by a certain date.

5. Start accumulating materials for the meeting. Sometimes it is helpful to have a large box, basket or cart. Make a check list of any necessary charts, reports, extra agendas, nametags and pens, blank note pads, your own note-taking necessities, etc..

6. Keep an up-to-date list of RSVP's and advise your supervisor of any feedback from others. These might include issues, ''secret'' agendas, desires for time or date change, etc. The more your manager can anticipate in advance, the better.

7. Plan to arrive early at the meeting site. Make sure that the room is clean, the temperature is comfortable, there are enough chairs, and all needed supplies are on hand. If your pre-planning has been thorough, there should not be any surprises. However, *something* usually needs adjustment, so:

8. Be sure to know where the nearest telephone is, and provide its number to someone in your office. (They may need to relay telephone calls to meeting participants, also.)

9. As participants arrive, give them nametags and other appropriate materials.

For an excellent book on meetings, order *EFFECTIVE MEETING SKILLS* by Elvin Haynes from the back of the book.

PLANNING FOR MEETINGS
(Continued)

10. Be ready to supply anything further that your supervisor may need as the meeting progresses.

11. Take notes, or have someone else do so.

12. At an appropriate time following the meeting (i.e. the next day), sit down with your supervisor and discuss how a similar meeting could be even better next time.

13. Keep a complete file on the meeting, including agenda, notes, lists of supplies, participants, and suggestions for improvement next time.

> PLANNING AND CREATING A SUCCESSFUL
> MEETING TAKES MANAGERIAL TALENT, TACT,
> AND HUMOR. THIS PART OF YOUR JOB CAN BE
> EXHAUSTING—BUT ALSO THE MOST FUN!

WHEN YOUR MANAGER TRAVELS TO A MEETING

Helping your manager prepare for a meeting away from the office is a breeze, compared to the responsibility of hosting one. Use the following checklist both before and after a meeting, conference, or convention. With a definite system, last-minute panic will be avoided.

BEFORE THE TRIP OR MEETING

—Start a folder for the trip as soon as you know one is scheduled.

—Collect information about meeting dates, transportation and/or lodging requirements, RSVP procedures, etc..

—Put in reminder slips of things your boss may wish to take along.

—Review what was in previous folders; check whether the same material is needed on this occasion.

—Make any necessary reservations for travel, meals or lodging.

—Before the meeting takes place, pretend you are "in your manager's shoes" and visualize what else might be needed.

—Make a list of everything taken to the meeting, and check things off when they are returned.

AFTER THE TRIP OR MEETING

—Review how the meeting arrangments went with your boss.

—Ask if additional data was needed for the meeting. Was it something you could have anticipated?

—Keep a folder of handouts, the agenda of the meeting, etc. Take action on any items requiring follow-up or a response.

—File the meeting folder and the "things needed" lists.

> YOUR MANAGER WILL THANK YOU FOR HELPING HIM/HER ORGANIZE CONFERENCE PAPERS. YOU BOTH MAY NEED THEM LATER WHEN PLANNING LONG-TERM GOALS OR WRITING REPORTS AND MEMOS.

REVIEW QUESTIONS FOR
SECTION III
YOUR ROLE AS OFFICE MANAGER

	ALWAYS	SOMETIMES	NEVER
1. Each day, I know my daily job priorities, and keep them in mind as I schedule work.			
2. I discuss my job priorities regularly with my supervisor.			
3. I plan definite timetables for big jobs, and stick to them to avoid last-minute crises.			
4. I group similar activities and do them together.			
5. I anticipate upcoming projects, so I am prepared to insure everything gets done ahead of time.			
6. I assist my manager in identifying long-term goals.			
7. I prepare a long-term goal calendar and check it regularly with my boss.			
8. I welcome the chance to make decisions, and base them on information I check and evaluate.			
9. I discuss upcoming decisions with people they affect and listen to their opinions and suggestions.			
10. To avoid work overload, I keep an assignment notebook and consult with my manager about conflicting priorities.			
11. When overload problems arise, I suggest sources of additional help.			
12. I try to attend courses and workshops regularly, in order to keep growing professionally.			

SECTION III REVIEW (Continued)

	ALWAYS	SOMETIMES	NEVER
13. When writing letters and memos, I keep my audience in mind and state a memo's main point in the first paragraph.			
14. When writing, I choose simple language rather than elaborate phrases or trade jargon.			
15. I view the telephone as an important customer service tool.			
16. I understand and practice telephone courtesy.			
17. When speaking in a business setting, I organize my thoughts in logical order.			
18. When arranging for meetings, I plan mailings, supplies, and room arrangements well in advance.			
19. After my manager attends a conference or meeting, I file all materials so they can be easily retrieved.			
20. I write down suggestions for improvement so future projects and/or meetings will be more productive.			

SECTION IV

YOUR ATTITUDE:
THE KEY TO SUCCESS WITH PEOPLE

In a recent study, The Research Institute of America reported that major career advancement for secretaries is based, first and foremost, on interpersonal skills. Technical skills and effort, although essential, were considered less important than good interpersonal skills.

Your ability to work with other people is your most valuable asset. Surveys show that top secretaries and associates have more contacts with people than any other individuals on the organization chart. This section presents a number of ways to improve your people-handling skills.

> The basis for every skill in this section is your ATTITUDE.
>
> To work well with others, you must feel good about yourself...and that feeling spreads outward, affecting everyone around you.

Of course, everyone has times when his or her attitude needs renewal, so a good place to start is with your attitude *today*.

Take out your pencil and give yourself the attitude assessment quiz on the next page...

ATTITUDE ADJUSTMENT SCALE

Rate your current attitude. Read the statement and circle the number where you feel you belong. If you circle a 10, you are saying your attitude could not be better in this area; if you circle a 1, you are saying it could not be worse. Be honest.

		HIGH (Positive)						LOW (Negative)			
1.	My feeling is that my boss would currently rate my attitude as:	10	9	8	7	6	5	4	3	2	1
2.	Given the same choice, my co-workers and family would rate my attitude as:	10	9	8	7	6	5	4	3	2	1
3.	Realistically, I would rate my attitude as:	10	9	8	7	6	5	4	3	2	1
4.	In dealing with others, I believe my effectiveness would rate:	10	9	8	7	6	5	4	3	2	1
5.	My current creativity level is:	10	9	8	7	6	5	4	3	2	1
6.	If there were a meter that could gauge my sense of humor I believe it would read:	10	9	8	7	6	5	4	3	2	1
7.	My recent disposition—the patience and sensitivity I show to others—deserves a rating of:	10	9	8	7	6	5	4	3	2	1
8.	When it comes to not allowing little things to bother me, I deserve a:	10	9	8	7	6	5	4	3	2	1
9.	Based upon the number of compliments I have received lately, I deserve a:	10	9	8	7	6	5	4	3	2	1
10.	I would rate my enthusiasm toward my job and life during the last few weeks as:	10	9	8	7	6	5	4	3	2	1

TOTAL _____

A score of 90 or over is a signal that your attitude is ''in tune'' and no adjustments seem necessary; a score between 70 and 90 indicates that minor adjustments may help; a rating between 50 and 70 suggests a major adjustment; if you rated yourself below 50, a complete overhaul may be required.

If the attitude adjustment scale showed you areas that could be improved, order ATTITUDE: YOUR MOST PRICELESS POSSESSION by Elwood N. Chapman (see the back of the book). It is filled with helpful exercises and suggestions for keeping a positive outlook in the workplace...and everywhere else in your life.

WHAT'S WRONG WITH BILL'S ATTITUDE?

Bill is a highly skilled secretary. He always completes his assignments rapidly and the quality of his work is among the best in the department. Unfortunately, Bill has a job that requires considerable interaction with others. He is intolerant of those who do not deliver the same quality of work he produces, and is not reluctant to express his opinion. His supervisor is considering changing his assignment because his attitude has caused co-workers to seek transfers to other departments. Despite his talent, Bill is a victim of his poor human relation skills.

What suggestions would you have for Bill? _____

_____

_____

_____

_____

_____

RELATIONSHIPS IN THE WORKPLACE

It is easy to assume that your same standards for friendship should be used for those with whom you work. WRONG! Work relationships exist for the purpose of getting jobs done. Whether or not a fellow worker is someone you would want as a friend has nothing to do with whether you can work together effectively and efficiently.

In organizations you will encounter people who have very different values or standards from your own. Here are some tips on building good relationships with all kinds of people:

1. Ask yourself: What is the purpose of our relationship?

2. Ask: Am I bringing a positive and open attitude toward this person?

3. Ask: What are the person's good qualities? How are they helpful to the organization?

4. If there is an open conflict, ask: What can I do to set things straight? (Attitude is more important here than any incident that created difficulty. There will always be incidents that are irritating. The only thing you have control over is your own attitude toward them!)

YOUR ATTITUDE SETS THE STAGE FOR WORK (AND PERSONAL) RELATIONSHIPS. REGARDLESS OF WHAT ACTUALLY HAPPENS, YOU ALWAYS HAVE THE CHOICE OF KEEPING A POSITIVE ATTITUDE.

UNDERSTANDING YOUR PERSONALITY

Dealing positively with other people depends on two aspects of personality:

1.   ASSERTIVENESS

2.   RECEPTIVENESS

When you understand yourself in these areas, you become more skillful in handling your many responsibilities at work.

ASSERTIVENESS

Let's first look at Assertiveness which can be defined as *being pleasantly direct.*

Do not mistake assertiveness with aggressiveness. When you are assertive you are being honest. Your attitude is "this is important to me and I am entitled to my opinion. At the same time, I respect that you are also entitled to your opinion."

The very nature of your work involves juggling a variety of duties. By your honest and direct communication with everyone, you gain energy...and do a better job.

NONASSERTIVE

ASSERTIVE

AGGRESSIVE

HOW ASSERTIVE ARE YOU?

By honestly answering the following questions, you will better understand your attitude toward assertiveness. An attitude, of course, does not always show up in behavior. You may *feel* more assertive than you *are* in real-life situations.

Circle T(true) or F(false):

1. T F I often feel like telling people what I really think of them.

2. T F When I find myself in a new situation, I watch what other people do and then try to act in a similar fashion.

3. T F I enjoy doing things that others may regard as unconventional.

4. T F I think it is important to learn obedience and practice correct social behavior.

5. T F In general, I find that I dislike non-conformists.

6. T F I prefer to listen to the opinion of others before I take a stand.

7. T F I feel comfortable following instructions and doing what is expected of me.

8. T F It often makes more sense to go along with ''the group'' rather than try to persuade them to my point of view.

9. T F Confronting other people is extremely uncomfortable for me.

10. T F I enjoy being seen as a person with strong opinions.

SCORING YOUR ASSERTIVENESS QUIZ

If you answered TRUE to items 2, 4, 5, 6, 7, 8, or 9, above give yourself one point for each. Also give one point for FALSE answers to items 1, 3, or 10, and total your points. If you scored 6 or more points, low assertiveness may be a problem for you. You may find yourself being far more reactive to the demands of others than you are to your own aspirations.

Many excellent books are available that can help you develop positive assertiveness. One of the best is DEVELOPING POSITIVE ASSERTIVENESS by Sam Lloyd which can be order from the back of the book.

HOW RECEPTIVE ARE YOU?

RECEPTIVENESS means being open to feedback. Obtaining feedback, even from your most severe critic, may be the most important way for you to gain direction and control. This feedback can lead to greater self-understanding. Read the following case, and respond to the questions:

FRANCES AND MARSHA

Frances, while eating lunch with her good friend Marsha, got on the subject of constructive criticism. Frances confided to Marsha that she was having difficulty understanding why her relationship with her boyfriend didn't seem to be going anywhere.

"If only he'd say what it is about me that doesn't appeal to him. I'd work on changing," Frances said, "but he just won't say. You're an old friend, Marsha. What do you think I'm doing wrong?"

Marsha had been waiting for this. Frances is a great person, but has some irritating behaviors. For example, she spends too much time complaining about things, but doesn't seem to make any changes to make things better. So, what the heck, Marsha thought, I'll tell her now while she seems to be looking for feedback.

"Frances," Marsha began, "You do have one trait that I find irritating, and maybe it bugs your boyfriend, too. You do an awful lot of complaining."

There was no response and Marsha thought Frances didn't seem too upset by what she'd said, so she continued: "In fact, it can be very depressing to be around you, because you always seem to complain about the same things—your boyfriend, your mother, your car—and yet you never seem to do anything to make things better. What I'd like to hear are some *good* things or some positive plans!"

Frances still wasn't responding and didn't even seem mad. After a pause, she started laughing out loud.

Then she said, "Marsha, do you realize that you just described perfectly *your own* habit of complaining? That's exactly why I try to avoid *you* sometimes."

Marsha was shocked. She wanted to just disappear for a moment. But then a lightbulb went on. Frances was right. The two women started laughing together.

"It looks like we both have something to work on!" said Marsha.

HOW RECEPTIVE ARE YOU?
(Continued)

QUESTIONS

1. What do you feel is the primary message of the case on the previous page?

_____

_____

_____

2. Do you think Marsha's observation was correct?

_____

_____

_____

3. Do you think Frances' response was appropriate?

_____

_____

_____

4. Is there a message in the case that you can personally relate to?

_____

_____

_____

(The facing page contains a feedback receptiveness quiz that relates directly to you.)

RECEPTIVENESS QUIZ

FEEDBACK RECEPTIVENESS QUIZ

Answer the following questions as honestly as possible. Do not share your answers.

As a general rule:

1. ( ) yes ( ) no I get embarrassed when people point out my mistakes.

2. ( ) yes ( ) no I resent people telling me what they think of my shortcomings.

3. ( ) yes ( ) no I regularly ask friends and associates I trust to comment on how I'm doing.

4. ( ) yes ( ) no I know how to offer constructive criticism to others in a sensitive way.

5. ( ) yes ( ) no I like people who tell me their reactions to my activities because it will help me adapt my future behavior.

Comments on Feedback Receptiveness

If you answered a definite "yes" to items 1 and 2 you may be putting up some attitude barriers that could deter you from obtaining useful feedback. We are normally uncomfortable when we receive harsh or insensitive feedback, but even that can be valuable, if we take it in perspective. Even our worst critic can provide a "gift" of good advice, if we don't allow the emotion of the moment to blind us.

Successful people learn how to develop an attitude of looking for a gem of good advice even when it's buried under a lot of worthless noise.

If you answered "yes" to items 3 and 4 you are creating a climate where helpful feedback is accepted and expected. Organizations fostering such a climate are typically positive places to work and successful in their results. In a similar fashion, individuals who foster an attitude of being "receptive" receive the benefit of input from others.

If you answered "yes" to item 5, you are probably a little unusual. But you're on the right track.

The preceding material on Assertiveness and Receptiveness was adapted from SUCCESSFUL SELF-MANAGEMENT, by Paul R. Timm, Ph.D. For order information, see the back of the book.

IDEALLY, THE PROFESSIONAL SECRETARY WILL KEEP A HEALTHY BALANCE BETWEEN *ASSERTIVENESS*
and
RECEPTIVENESS.

Your *assertiveness* enables you to set priorities, organize your time and energies, and let others know that you are a serious professional.

When you are active, direct, and honest, you communicate self-respect and respect for others. People know where *you* stand, and trust you to listen to *their* point of view.

Your *receptiveness* helps you listen and *really hear what you need to know* about other people's needs and priorities. Even when people say things that are critical or unpleasant, you maintain your poise and use the information to help you do a better job.

BUILDING A NETWORK

Without realizing it, you have probably already built a *network* of professional colleagues who are willing to help and advise you. Your network consists of people both inside and outside of your organization who know you and your work. Key associates in your network keep you abreast of "what's happening." They may be in the same industry or field as you, or they may give you tips on developments in unrelated fields.

Why do you need a network?

—To give and receive support, advice, and insight.

—To exchange specific information about trends, personnel changes and career opportunities.

—To transact business, or get a (perhaps new or unfamiliar) job done

Networking is a two-way street. When you invest time and energy in other people, they become valuable allies when you, in turn, need support or information. This is called a mutually rewarding relationship.

Are you setting up a conference? Putting out a newsletter? Re-organizing a department? Making a major office purchase? These are occasions when you can use your network. Why re-invent the wheel when you can consult others who have faced the same challenges?

HOW TO BUILD A NETWORK AND KEEP IT ALIVE

1. Always ask (and write down for future reference) the name of someone who has proven helpful with a project. Tell that person you would be glad to reciprocate, should the need arise.

2. If you meet someone whose work really impresses you, ask about his or her background, what training courses or materials have been useful, what reading he/she recommends, etc.

3. Send letters of praise or congratulations to people in your office or industry who receive honors or special recognition, maybe even to people you have never met.

4. A planned ''Open House'' for your office can be a welcome surprise—and lead to warmer contacts with other departments, suppliers, clients, outside sales representatives, etc.

5. If your organization encourages public service involvement, volunteer—it's a great way to meet people you would not ordinarily see.

6. If you need (or desire) further training or education to meet your goals, find someone to advise and direct you.

7. Learn to draw an organizational chart of your company. Make a bargain with yourself to develop at least one contact from every major part of it!

8. Join a trade/industry group appropriate to your organization.

9. Don't forget your personal network. Maybe you have friends or family members who could give you useful professional advice. Ask them!

RESOLVING CONFLICT IN YOUR OFFICE

Conflict is inevitable whether an office consists of two people or ten thousand people. However, with your attitude tuned to "positive", your value as a problem solver *among people* has unlimited potential.

Here are some standard sources of conflict found in the workplace. For each category, write a brief example of conflict you have personally observed:

SOURCES OF CONFLICT

—An organization whose structure encourages conflict (perhaps by making workers compete against each other for special rewards).

(Your example) _____

—Aggressive co-workers _____

—Competition for resources (i.e. only one computer for three workers)

_____

—Power struggles (i.e. who will head the new department)

_____

—Organizational change (People use many tricks to avoid changing comfortable routines)

_____

—Unresolved previous conflicts (even when the current issue should present no problems, previous grudges may interfere)

_____

—DIFFERENCES in
  Facts and assumptions _____
  Customs and habits _____
  Goals and expectations _____
  Roles _____
  Methods and styles _____

RESOLVING CONFLICT (6 EASY STEPS)

Anticipating conflict (and knowing its causes, as you just listed) is one of the best ways of heading off a situation *before it erupts*. When a conflict exists, either for you, or among people in your organization, try using the following steps to maintain a positive environment.

1. **Schedule a meeting with the other party.** Decide on a time and place to sit down and discuss differences. That way you have each made a gesture toward resolution. *Example: Debra, your department bookkeeper, resists your requests for statistics you need to include in regular reports. Think about the ideal time and place to meet with her, and say, "We need to talk about our working relationship and how it can be improved."*

2. **Evaluate the cause.** First acknowledge that there is a conflict. (Not admitting there's a problem makes it worse.) Talk non-judgmentally about the reasons for your differences.

3. **Use "I" messages.** Say "I thought you wanted this," or "I heard you to say that." In this way, you avoid destructive accusations. Here is a pattern for an "I" message:

I _____ when you _____ which causes _____
    (feel, react)   (act, do)

_____
(consequences)

4. **Encourage the other person to express his or her feelings.** Ask questions that draw out what the other person is thinking. Use phrases like "I would like your reaction to what happened," or "I would like to hear your reasons." In our example, the bookkeeper might say that she had no idea of the importance of the reports you worked on, or who needed the figures. She might also point out that you are often late giving her the information she needs for the report. The idea is to let the other party know that you are *truly listening carefully to his or her opinions.*

5. **Structure your desired outcome.** Negotiate! Be sure that you each contribute to the "solution" and feel satisfied that it is at least worth trying. (Not every problem is going to be solved overnight but progress can usually be made, even on those that are most difficult.) Some people like to write down agreements; but for most office situations, a handshake symbolizes mutual respect and agreement to work toward a solution.

6. **Evaluate.** It's a good idea to set a definite time in the future (a week, a month, etc.) to evaluate the solution.

> When you successfully negotiate a conflict, using the above guidelines, you will be amazed at how powerful you feel! Your power is *not* to push other people around, but to improve communications with those who may have different views.

For an excellent book on conflict resolution order MANAGING DISAGREEMENT CONSTRUCTIVELY by Herbert S. Kindler, Ph.D. from page 73.

CONFLICT RESOLUTION EXERCISE

Answer the following questions:

With whom do you have (or currently have) a conflict?

What is the essence of this conflict?

1. _____   _____

2. _____   _____

3. _____   _____

4. _____   _____

5. _____   _____

Choose one of your examples and complete the following questions:

1) How could you apply the "Six steps of conflict resolution" (explained on the two previous pages) for this conflict?

2) What happens if you choose not to express yourself?

YOU AND YOUR MANAGER;
A Very Special Relationship

Normally you will not instantly establish a special working relationship with your manager. Like most other relationships, it will develop over time. The quality of the ultimate working relationship will be made up of countless small incidents which demonstrate to each of you what to expect from the other.

Your professional abilities are important. But even more significant is your desire to carry out your tasks in a way that "fits" with your manager's goals and style.

WHAT MAKES A GOOD MANAGER?

Secretaries who are most satisfied with their jobs and managers list the following reasons:

1. A manager who shows respect and fairness toward all employees.
2. A person who builds mutual rapport and trust, and is willing to share ideas and goals.
3. One who has the qualities of a good teacher, i.e. clarity and patience when delegating new tasks.
4. A person who will delegate with trust, but who also monitors assignments and provides helpful feedback.
5. A boss who meets regularly with you (preferably daily) to set priorities and goals.
6. One who encourages everyone to seek improvements in office functions and procedures and *listens* when improvements are suggested.
7. An individual who is accessible on a regular basis, despite a frantic schedule or problems in certain departments. (One who does not "blow up" in anger very often.)
8. A well mannered person who says "thank you" and shows special appreciation for extra effort.

CAN YOU ADD OTHER FACTORS WHICH IDENTIFY A GOOD MANAGER?

_____

_____

_____

HOW DOES YOUR MANAGER RATE? Over time, you can influence your manager's behavior and attitude by *modeling* professional behavior.
Remember: your attitude affects everyone around you...especially your boss!

CHECKLIST FOR ESTABLISHING GOOD RAPPORT WITH YOUR MANAGER

☐ 1. Observe his/her natural pace of work, and adjust your methods accordingly. Tension results when you do not understand priorities; try to figure these out as soon as possible.

☐ 2. Most managers need you to act as a buffer between them and the telephone or unexpected visitors. Learn which people are welcome at any time, and which should be screened or helped by you.

☐ 3. Open channels of communication, especially about "little" things such as the preferred way of answering the phone, whether or not your manager always wants you to ask who is calling, whether he/she wants to let anyone else take material out of certain files, etc.

☐ 4. Realize that *you* often know more than your manager about certain incidents, procedures, and/or relationships in the workplace. Keep your manager informed about things which are important.

☐ 5. "Save" your manager when he/she drafts a letter or memo in anger or when an important paper is misplaced. You might delay sending an angry letter for a day, and then have your manager read it for "errors." With the lost paper, think of ways it might have been incorrectly filed, and help with the search. (Keep a chronological file of every key paper coming in and going out: this has solved many crises.)

☐ 6. Stay within your authority. Do not use your manager's status as a way of pushing other people around. The more important your manager, of course, the greater your own power. But if you abuse it, it will reflect poorly on both of you. (Example: If your manager asks you to tell someone to turn in a report at their earliest convenience, don't say, "My boss wants this immediately!")

☐ 7. Help your manager keep to his/her schedule. Work out a method for you to interrupt long-winded visitors or telephone callers without offending anyone.

☐ 8. Above all, protect and preserve your manager's faith in your loyalty. Your manager's (and your) reputation can rest on your ability to keep information private and confidential.

REVIEW QUESTIONS FOR SECTION IV: ATTITUDE: THE SECRETARY'S KEY TO SUCCESS WITH PEOPLE

TRUE OR FALSE?

T   **F**

_____   _____   1. Career advancement for a secretary depends more on technical skills than interpersonal skills.

_____   _____   2. A person's attitude influences every personal and professional relationship.

_____   _____   3. You should judge your fellow workers using the same standards you use for friends.

_____   _____   4. Regardless of what actually happens, you always have the choice of keeping a positive attitude.

_____   _____   5. "Assertiveness" means being pleasantly direct.

_____   _____   6. "Receptiveness" means being open to feedback.

_____   _____   7. Success usually means you have a good balance between receptiveness and assertiveness.

_____   _____   8. If people are helpful to you in your work, there is no need to learn their names.

_____   _____   9. It takes time, organization, and effort to build a "network."

_____   _____   10. A person's network consists of people both inside and outside the organization.

_____   _____   11. Conflict is inevitable.

_____   _____   12. In resolving conflict, it is very important to listen to the other person's opinions and perceptions.

_____   _____   13. An "I" message tells how you see or understand something, without blaming the other person.

_____   _____   14. The more important your supervisor, the less need to consider other people's opinions.

_____   _____   15. A manager must believe in your loyalty and ability to protect private information.

ANSWERS: All true, except for 1, 3, 8, and 14.

SECTION V:
THE FINISHING TOUCH

As your professional skills grow, it is normal for you to see yourself differently. Your outward appearance and personal habits may change. This section will provide some examples of "finishing touches" that make the difference between a secretary and a professional secretary.

LOOK PROFESSIONAL

The first thing anyone notices about you is how you look. We all know, too, that how we look affects how we feel. Our self-image definitely influences our *attitude*. Therefore:

> TO BECOME A PROFESSIONAL SUCCESS, LOOK LIKE A SUCCESS...EVERY DAY. YOU NEVER HAVE A SECOND CHANCE TO MAKE A FIRST IMPRESSION.

The specifics of what is in fashion and appropriate vary from place to place, year by year. But you can always observe professionally-dressed people in your own office or on the street, making note of styles and colors which seem appropriate for you. (Also observe those details which label a person as unprofessional.)

Consider how you can use the following elements to enhance the image you want to project:

1. Simplicity
2. Elegance
3. Orderliness

THESE ELEMENTS APPLY TO YOUR HAIRSTYLE AS WELL AS YOUR CLOTHING. YOUR CLOTHES MAKE A STATEMENT ABOUT YOU: DRESS THE PART YOU WOULD LIKE TO PLAY IN YOUR PROFESSIONAL WORLD.

(At this point, you may wonder if you have to throw out everything you now own. Certainly not. But don't wear inappropriate clothing *to the office*. If it turns out that you honestly have only three outfits appropriate for a professional person in your office, rotate those outfits until you can add more pieces.)

62

LOOKING PROFESSIONAL

HOW TO SABOTAGE YOUR IMAGE

1. Buy cheap clothing.

2. Wear worn-out or soiled clothing.

3. Look sloppy.

4. Dress too "cutesy," too "gadgety." Anything that is "too" anything.

5. Emphasize your worst features.

6. Minimize your good physical features.

7. Disregard your grooming (hair not combed, fingernails dirty, etc.).

8. Improperly match and blend items in your wardrobe.

9. Wear inappropriate accessories—things that stand out garishly, such as cheap jewelry.

10. Dress inappropriately for the occasion—casual when you should appear elegant or vice-versa.

11. Dress without any flair—always dull and uninteresting, uninspired, always the same.

12. Dress inappropriately for your age.

13. Ignore your personal habits (gum chewing, body odor, bad breath, etc.)

14. Follow the latest fashion trends blindly, obediently and thoughtlessly.

15. Allow clothing clerks to sell you, rather than serve you.

NONVERBAL COMMUNICATION OR BODY LANGUAGE

This is what others remember about you long after they have forgotten what you said. It has been proven that 65% of all communication is nonverbal!

Think about the following elements and observe the people in your own office. Then, pledge that the rest of your working life, you will make *your* nonverbal communication say "professional."

HANDSHAKE — Both men and women should have a firm, steady handshake! This shows self-confidence and a willingness to communicate.

APPROPRIATE OR INAPPROPRIATE LAUGHTER — This is a very individual trait. In general, however, it is better to curtail loud horselaughs and foolish giggling in a business setting. Excessive laughter usually indicates nervousness.

FACIAL EXPRESSIONS — "Mugging" and "wide-eyed child" faces grow tiresome very quickly.

RATE OF SPEECH — Slower is better than faster, especially on the telephone.

POSTURE — The professional person looks calm, relaxed, yet ready for work and challenge. This means standing, sitting, and moving with grace. Don't slouch, twist, or contort yourself, especially when typing or word processing.

GESTURES — These can emphasize your point when appropriate, but too many gestures can make other people uncomfortable.

EYE CONTACT — Maintain eye contact with the person to whom you are speaking. If you are sitting, turn around and face the person fully.

YOUR IMAGE IS A PICTURE—A PORTRAIT. WHAT YOU WEAR, SAY AND DO FORMS AN OVERALL IMPRESSION. MAKE YOURS PROFESSIONAL!

PERSONAL HABITS

Check whether the following are appropriate in an office setting:

Yes   No

1. Obscene language

2. Gum chewing

3. Run-down heels, scuffed shoes

4. Nylon stockings for women, ties for men

5. Long personal phone conversations

6. Eating at your desk

7. Sunglasses

8. Clothing mended with safety pins

9. Sports outfits

10. Application of make-up, lotions

It's pretty obvious that only #4 would rate a ''yes'' on this list!

What personal habits do you *appreciate* in fellow workers?

1. _____

2. _____

3. _____

SHOULD YOU DECORATE YOUR OFFICE?

Think carefully about this! Do not bring anything into your work area until you have been with the organization awhile. Think twice before you install:

1. Too many plants

2. A gallery of family snapshots

3. Children's artworks

4. Decorations of any kind

Ask yourself: Do other professionals in this office display personal items? What do I want my decorations to say about me? Do I want to "share" my personal life with everyone who comes into the office?

Sometimes one personal item of yours will be so odd or unusual that it is the only thing remembered about you. An office-mate of one of the authors taped "the first dollar she ever made" to the wall by her desk.

Should the dollar bill have been taped to the wall? Why?

_____

_____

What personal decorations do you think are appropriate in an office setting?

_____

_____

_____

_____

_____

THE FINISHING TOUCH
Section Review

Check TRUE or FALSE for each statement.

TRUE   **FALSE**

_____ _____ 1. The first thing anyone notices about you is how you look.

_____ _____ 2. It's O.K. to wear sports clothes on the days the boss won't be in the office.

_____ _____ 3. You should throw out any unprofessional clothes in your closet.

_____ _____ 4. It's always safe to follow the latest fashion trends.

_____ _____ 5. If you are discreet, it is O.K. to chew gum and/or eat "munchies" at your desk.

_____ _____ 6. You don't need a firm handshake.

_____ _____ 7. The faster your rate of speaking, the more businesslike you sound.

_____ _____ 8. When speaking to someone, look over the person's shoulder to avoid embarrassment.

_____ _____ 9. On your first day of work, bring in a box of personal possessions to decorate your own space.

_____ _____ 10. Your professional image is a portrait of how you look, speak, and behave.

ANSWERS: The first and last statements are true. 2-9 are false.

SECTION VI:

SUMMARY CHECKLIST FOR THE PROFESSIONAL SECRETARY

Working toward professional excellence, for a secretary, leads in many directions!
The checklist on the following page will help you analyze your job performance
and set goals for future growth.

CHECKLIST FOR SUCCESS

WHEN CONSIDERING MY JOB, I WILL

—Identify how my job fits into the organization as a whole.

—Describe the "service" my office provides.

—Look for ways to do my job more effectively.

TO ASSESS MY PROFESSIONAL GOALS AND IMAGE, I WILL:

—Determine my career goals.

—Begin changing my daily behaviors in order to achieve professional growth.

IN MY ROLE AS OFFICE MANAGER I WILL:

—Survey my daily tasks and begin setting priorities.

—Avoid procrastination and dependence on non-existent "catch up" time.

—Determine several important long-range goals for my office and block out periods of time to work on them.

—Practice making decisions by considering a variety of alternatives, rating them, and then taking action.

—Set up a system to record work assignments and to get help when overloaded.

—Learn about career-building classes in my area.

—Write letters and memos only after considering (1) the audience, and (2) the simplest, quickest way to state the message.

—Realize that every phone call can deliver quality customer service.

—Plan impromptu speeches by breaking the subject matter into logical parts, and summarizing main points at the end.

—Create checklists for planning, evaluating, and following-up after meetings.

CHECKLIST FOR SUCCESS
(Continued)

TO BUILD GOOD WORKING RELATIONSHIPS I WILL:

—See office relationships as a chance to listen to and learn about a wide variety of other people.

—Practice expressing my own opinions and decisions in a friendly, positive manner.

—Build a network of helpful colleagues, both inside and outside my organization, who could contribute to my success.

—Recognize that conflict occurs whenever people work together and practice discussing and resolving issues as they arise.

—Arrange my work schedule to best meet my manager's needs, remaining flexible enough to accommodate unexpected changes.

TO COMPLETE MY PROFESSIONAL IMAGE I WILL:

—Choose clothing and accessories that are appropriate for professionals in my office.

—Be conscious of my nonverbal communications—i.e. posture, eye contact, personal habits—keep them in tune with the rest of my image.

—Assess the appearance of my work area and see it as an extension of my professional portrait.

PERSONAL ACTION PLAN

MY PERSONAL ACTION PLAN AND COMMITMENT TO POSITIVE CHANGE

The best intentions in the world lead nowhere unless they are put into action. By completing this book, you have said ''yes'' to career growth. The next step is putting your plans into writing and setting up a time schedule.

Using the Summary Checklist on the two previous pages, select *three* ''I Will'' statements which would help you perform your job in a more professional manner. Then, after each statement, write how you will fulfill your goal, and one (or more) steps you could take *tomorrow* to begin.

(EXAMPLE: I will set up a system to record work assignments and to get help when overloaded. *Possible methods:* I will purchase a notebook, setting up columns for the date, the assignments, their projected time requirements, and their due dates. Then I will discuss the usefulness of the notebook with my manager, and suggest ways of obtaining assistance when needed. *What I can do tomorrow:* Purchase the notebook, set up the columns, possibly have the discussion with my manager.)

YOUR GOALS

1. I will _____

Method: _____

_____

_____

Tomorrow I will _____

_____

_____

2. I will _____

_____

_____

Method: _____

_____

_____

Tomorrow I will _____

_____

_____

_____

3. I will _____

_____

_____

Method: _____

_____

_____

_____

Tomorrow I will _____

_____

_____

_____

When you regularly repeat this method of goal-setting, you will feel your attitude improve and your energy increase. Keep this book handy and use it for recording your goals. Good luck!

THE FIFTY-MINUTE SERIES

Quantity	Title	Code #	Price	Amount
	MANAGEMENT TRAINING			
	Successful Negotiation	09-2	$7.95	
	Personal Performance Contracts	12-2	$7.95	
	Team Building	16-5	$7.95	
	Effective Meeting Skills	33-5	$7.95	
	An Honest Day's Work	39-4	$7.95	
	Managing Disagreement Constructively	41-6	$7.95	
	Training Managers To Train	43-2	$7.95	
	The Fifty-Minute Supervisor	58-0	$7.95	
	Leadership Skills For Women	62-9	$7.95	
	Problem Solving & Decision Making	63-7	$7.95	
	Coaching & Counseling For Supervisors	68-8	$7.95	
	Management Dilemmas: A Guide to Business Ethics	69-6	$7.95	
	Understanding Organizational Change	71-8	$7.95	
	Project Management	75-0	$7.95	
	Managing Organizational Change	80-7	$7.95	
	Managing A Diverse Workforce	85-8	$7.95	
	PERSONNEL TRAINING & HUMAN RESOURCE MANAGEMENT			
	Effective Performance Appraisals	11-4	$7.95	
	Quality Interviewing	13-0	$7.95	
	Personal Counseling	14-9	$7.95	
	Job Performance and Chemical Dependency	27-0	$7.95	
	New Employee Orientation	46-7	$7.95	
	Professional Excellence for Secretaries	52-1	$7.95	
	Guide To Affirmative Action	54-8	$7.95	
	Writing A Human Resource Manual	70-X	$7.95	
	COMMUNICATIONS			
	Effective Presentation Skills	24-6	$7.95	
	Better Business Writing	25-4	$7.95	
	The Business of Listening	34-3	$7.95	
	Writing Fitness	35-1	$7.95	
	The Art of Communicating	45-9	$7.95	
	Technical Presentation Skills	55-6	$7.95	
	Making Humor Work For You	61-0	$7.95	
	Better Technical Writing	64-5	$7.95	
	Using Visual Aids in Business	77-7	$7.95	
	Influencing Others: A Practical Guide	84-X	$7.95	
	SELF-MANAGEMENT			
	Balancing Home And Career	10-6	$7.95	
	Mental Fitness: A Guide to Emotional Health	15-7	$7.95	
	Personal Financial Fitness	20-3	$7.95	
	Attitude: Your Most Priceless Possession	21-1	$7.95	
	Personal Time Management	22-X	$7.95	

(Continued on next page)

THE FIFTY-MINUTE SERIES

Quantity	Title	Code #	Price	Amount
	SELF-MANAGEMENT (CONTINUED)			
	Preventing Job Burnout	23-8	$7.95	
	Successful Self-Management	26-2	$7.95	
	Developing Positive Assertiveness	38-6	$7.95	
	Time Management And The Telephone	53-X	$7.95	
	Memory Skills In Business	56-4	$7.95	
	Developing Self-Esteem	66-1	$7.95	
	Creativity In Business	67-X	$7.95	
	Quality Awareness: A Personal Guide To Professional Standards	72-6	$7.95	
	Managing Personal Change	74-2	$7.95	
	Speedreading For Better Productivity	78-5	$7.95	
	Winning At Human Relations	86-6	$7.95	
	Stop Procrastinating	88-2	$7.95	
	SALES TRAINING/QUALITY CUSTOMER SERVICE			
	Sales Training Basics	02-5	$7.95	
	Restaurant Server's Guide	08-4	$7.95	
	Quality Customer Service	17-3	$7.95	
	Telephone Courtesy And Customer Service	18-1	$7.95	
	Professional Selling	42-4	$7.95	
	Customer Satisfaction	57-2	$7.95	
	Telemarketing Basics	60-2	$7.95	
	Calming Upset Customers	65-3	$7.95	
	Managing A Quality Service Organization	83-1	$7.95	
	ENTREPRENEURSHIP			
	Marketing Your Consulting Or Professional Services	40-8	$7.95	
	Starting Your Small Business	44-0	$7.95	
	Publicity Power	82-3	$7.95	
	CAREER GUIDANCE & STUDY SKILLS			
	Study Skills Strategies	05-X	$7.95	
	Career Discovery	07-6	$7.95	
	Plan B: Protecting Your Career From The Winds of Change	48-3	$7.95	
	I Got The Job!	59-9	$7.95	
	OTHER CRISP INC. BOOKS			
	Comfort Zones: A Practical Guide For Retirement Planning	00-9	$13.95	
	Stepping Up To Supervisor	11-8	$13.95	
	The Unfinished Business Of Living: Helping Aging Parents	19-X	$12.95	
	Managing Performance	23-7	$18.95	
	Be True To Your Future: A Guide to Life Planning	47-5	$13.95	
	Up Your Productivity	49-1	$10.95	
	How To Succeed In A Man's World	79-3	$7.95	
	Practical Time Management	275-4	$13.95	
	Copyediting: A Practical Guide	51-3	$18.95	

THE FIFTY-MINUTE SERIES
(Continued)

☐ Send volume discount information.

☐ Please send me a catalog.

	Amount
Total (from other side)	
Shipping ($1.50 first book, $.50 per title thereafter)	
California Residents add 7% tax	
Total	

Ship to: _____

_____

_____

_____

Phone number: _____

Bill to: _____

_____

_____

_____

P.O. # _____

**All orders except those with a P.O.# must be prepaid.
For more information Call (415) 949-4888 or FAX (415) 949-1610.**

NO POSTAGE
NECESSARY
IF MAILED
IN THE
UNITED STATES

BUSINESS REPLY

FIRST CLASS   PERMIT NO. 884   LOS ALTOS, CA

POSTAGE WILL BE PAID BY ADDRESSEE

Crisp Publications, Inc.
95 First Street
Los Altos, CA 94022